GW00854833

Top 10 T...

for

Christmas

by

Lydia Reeves and Imogen Reeves

clean
eating

Copyright © Clean Eating 2015

Contents

Introduction

Christmas can be a very tempting time of year for all of us. It is very easy to suddenly find yourself submerged in a full blown Christmas sugar frenzy! If you desperately want to keep your health on track, but know that Christmas is always your downfall, now it can be a little easier to stay healthy throughout the festive season.

My name is Lydia. Over the last few years I have been on my own clean eating journey and have fixed all sorts of health issues that I had always thought would be with me for life. Now I am healthier and happier than I ever imagined I could be and I am passionate about helping other people who also want to make healthier choices for themselves or their families.

I have collaborated with my sister Imogen, and together we have picked our top 10 favourite Christmas treats. Our Clean Eating kitchens turned into mess and mayhem while we created super tasty, good-for-you variations to share. They're healthy, Christmassy, guilt-free goodies packed with deliciousness! What's not to love?!

These recipes are created to satisfy your sweet tooth over Christmas, whilst keeping you healthy and energised. We even challenge you to make them for your friends and family, and if they can notice all the goodness packed into them we'll eat our Santa hats!

All our recipes are gluten, dairy and refined sugar free, making these treats a guilt-free but delicious alternative to the sugar filled snacks that leave you feeling dozy, bloated and sluggish. Most of our recipes are also vegan, look out for the Ⓥ next to the treat title.

And one extra bonus, you'll be well on your way to your 'must eat healthier' New Year's resolution, before the New Year! And long may it continue!

We hope you have a very happy, healthy Christmas!

Love,
Lydia and Imogen

Hazelnut Chocolate Treats (makes 12) Ⓥ

Simple and delicious! It is hard to believe these have only 3 ingredients and no sugar! Roasting the hazelnuts first is a must to give them their full indulgent flavour.

Ingredients

- 1 cup hazelnuts (130g)
- ½ cup pitted dates roughly chopped (80g)
- 1 tbsp cocoa powder

Method

- Soak the dates in water for 1 hour to soften.
- Roast the hazelnuts in a preheated oven at 180°C for 12 minutes (make sure to check on them so they don't burn!)
- Allow to cool then rub in folded kitchen paper to remove the skins.
- Blend the dates, ½ a cup of hazelnuts and the cocoa powder in a food processor.
- Place whole hazelnut in the centre of a ball of mixture, continue making balls until all mixture is used.
- Chop remaining hazelnuts for the coating, then roll the balls over the chopped nuts.
- Chill in freezer for 30 minutes before serving.

Merry Mince Pies (makes 12) Ⓥ

We still can't quite believe how yummy these are! We may be a tiny bit biased, but they're so much more delicious than the supermarket, sugar-filled sort.

Ingredients

For filling:
- 1 cup mixed sultanas, currants, and raisins (120g)
- ½ cup chopped pitted dates (80g)
- 1 chopped apple
- Zest and flesh of 1 orange
- 2 tsp ground cinnamon
- 2 tsp ground ginger
- ½ tsp nutmeg

For pastry:
- 2 cups gluten-free flour (280g)
- 2 tbsp soft coconut oil (60g)
- 1½ tbsp dairy-free spread (50g)
- 2 tsp ground ginger
- 2 tsp ground cinnamon
- 1 tsp nutmeg
- 8-10 tbsp of water

Method

- To make the pastry, sieve the flour into a bowl and add the spices, spread and coconut oil. Mix with your hands until it forms crumbs. Add water gradually and knead mixture until a ball of dough forms. Chill for 30 minutes.
- To make the filling, blend the apple, dates, orange zest and flesh in a food processor. Empty into a bowl and mix in the dried fruits and spices.
- Preheat the oven to 180°C. Place pastry between two sheets of baking paper and roll out until 3mm thick. Cut pastry bases with a circle cutter slightly larger than the tin size and line your tins with it, pushing the pastry up the edges.
- Spoon the mixture into each pastry case then cut smaller lids out of remaining pastry. Wet the edges of lids with water and attach to bases, pinching together to seal. Pierce lids with knife to allow steam out
- Bake for 15 minutes. Cool slightly before removing from the tin and placing on cooling rack. Best eaten the same day!

Orange and Coconut Cookies (makes 10) Ⓥ

These crumbly coconut cookies are one of our favourites, and we always make double as they disappear so quickly! If you somehow have any left over, make sure you leave one out for Santa!

Ingredients
- ½ cup gluten free oats (45g)
- ½ cup pitted dates roughly chopped (80g)
- ½ cup sesame seeds (70g)
- ½ cup desiccated coconut (40g)
- Zest and juice of 1 orange
- 1½ tbsp soft coconut oil
- ¾ tbsp dairy-free spread

Method
- Blend all dry ingredients in a food processor until crumbly.
- Put mixture in a bowl and mix in the orange juice, zest, coconut oil and spread.
- Line a baking tray with baking paper, shape into flat circles and cook for 15 minutes at 160°C or until golden brown.

Mini Christmas Puds (makes 2)

These are made in individual pudding basins found in cook shops. Or, if you have any around, use the plastic pots left from last years Christmas puddings! These puds are full of flavour and make perfect individual desserts.

Ingredients

- ¾ cup pitted dates roughly chopped (120g)
- Zest of 1 orange, juice of ½ orange
- ¼ cup coconut oil (25g)
- 1 cup ground almonds (80g)
- 1 cup mixed sultanas, raisins and currants (210g)

- 1½ tsp all spice
- 1½ tsp ground cinnamon
- ½ tsp nutmeg
- 1 tbsp honey
- 1 egg

Method

- Melt coconut oil. Blend dates, orange juice and coconut oil in blender.
- Mix the date mixture with the rest of the ingredients in a bowl.
- Push into individual pudding basins (150ml) and cover in baking paper and then tin foil. Put an elastic band around the top so no water gets in.
- Place in large pan and add water until the level reaches half way up the puddings basins. Cover the pan with a lid and boil for 1 hour, check half way through and top up water if needed.
- Take out of water and unwrap carefully. Slide knife around edge to loosen and then turn upside-down. Best served warm.

Little Gingerbread Men (makes 2 trays worth)

These lil' guys are almost too cute to eat. They make perfect office snacks, party nibbles, or just delicious little treats to have in the house!

Ingredients

- 2 cups ground almonds (200g)
- ½ cup pitted dates roughly chopped (80g)
- 1 tsp ground cinnamon
- ¼ tsp ground nutmeg
- 2 tsp ground ginger
- ½ tsp gluten free baking powder
- 3 tbsp cold pressed olive oil, macadamia or coconut oil
- 2 tbsp honey, maple syrup, or agave nectar
- 1 egg white

Method

- Combine ground almonds, dates and spices in a food processor. Process until mix is crumbly.
- Pour into a mixing bowl and add oil, honey, and egg white. Mix until a soft dough forms.
- Roll the dough between 2 pieces of baking paper until 3mm thick. Refrigerate for 1 hour to allow the dough to firm up. If in a hurry, place in the freezer for 20 minutes.
- Cut into shapes, decorate with nuts, seeds or currants (optional) and place cookies onto a baking tray lined with baking paper. Bake at 150°C for 20 minutes or until golden brown. Remove from the oven and cool.

Figgy Slices (makes 12) Ⓥ

As well as these fig slices, this recipe could also make a delicious yule log. Follow the steps to make the mixture, then just roll the whole log in coconut and only slice when it is being served!

Ingredients
- 1 cup dried figs (150g)
- ½ cup raisins (80g)
- 1 cup gluten free oats (90g)
- ¾ cup desiccated coconut (60g) (¼ cup of this (20g) saved for topping)
- ½ cup sunflower seeds (65g)

Method
- Place figs, raisins, oats and ½ cup coconut into food processor. Process until mixture lifts away from edge.
- Remove from processor and knead sunflower seeds into mixture.
- Form a log and slice into 12 even slices
- Press each slice in remaining coconut.

Chocolate Orange Mousse (makes 2) Ⓥ

This smooth and creamy chocolate pudding is a secretly healthy alternative to a traditional dessert. Serve this after dinner and no one will even know it is full of goodness too (unless you 'wow' them with your culinary secrets of course!)

Ingredients
- 2 ripe avocados
- Juice and zest of 2 oranges
- ½ cup pitted dates roughly chopped (80g)
- 2 tbsp cocoa powder

Method
- Soak dates in water for 1 hour to soften.
- Blend the avocado, dates, cocoa powder, orange juice and half of the orange zest in a blender until smooth.
- Decant into bowls.
- Add the rest of the orange zest as a topping.
- Chill in the fridge before serving, or eat straight away!

Clean Christmas Cake

This fruit cake makes the best Christmas cake. It is so jam-packed with flavours! You can decorate it with a sprig of holly, nuts, or honey glazed fruits. It is the perfect dessert after an indulgent Christmas dinner.

Ingredients

- 3½ cups mixed dried fruit (raisins, sultanas, chopped prunes, figs, apricot and dates) (600g)
- 2 cups ground almonds (190g)
- ½ cup walnuts (50g)
- Juice and zest of 1 orange
- 3 eggs
- 1 tsp ground cinnamon
- 1 tsp vanilla bean extract
- ¼ tsp nutmeg
- 3 tbsp oil

Method

- Preheat oven to 150°C. Line cake tin with baking paper.
- Combine dried fruit, cinnamon, vanilla, orange zest & juice, oil and eggs in a mixing bowl.
- Mix in almonds and walnuts.
- Spoon mixture into a deep, 7" round cake tin and cover with baking paper to prevent burning. Bake for 1 hour. Remove paper and bake for further 15 minutes. If a skewer doesn't come out clean, bake for another 15 minutes. Allow to cool and remove from tin.

Sweet Shortbread (makes 16) Ⓥ

This shortbread alternative is sweetened with dates rather than sugar. It can be a soft biscuit or double baked for a crispier version. Relax in front of the fire with a hot cuppa and a guilt-free shortbread. In these dark evenings we couldn't think of anything better!

Ingredients

- 2 cups ground almonds (190g)
- ½ cup pitted dates roughly chopped (80g)
- ½ tsp salt
- ¼ tsp baking soda
- ¼ cup melted coconut oil (55g)
- 2 tsp vanilla extract
- 1 tbsp tinned coconut milk

Method

- Soak dates in water for 1 hour to soften.
- Line a 10" x 7" baking tray with baking paper and preheat oven to 160°C
- Blend the dates in food processor then mix with coconut oil, vanilla and coconut milk.
- In a separate bowl mix ground almonds with salt and baking soda.
- Add all ingredients together and mix well.
- Push dough into tin and prick with a fork. For best results chill over night, then bake for 20 minutes.
- Leave to cool completely before slicing. These will now be soft biscuits.
- If you would like them crispier, bake again for another 25 minutes at 120°C.

Blueberry and Orange Cheesecake ⓥ

Cashews work wonders to create a delicious creamy texture. There is no way you would think this was dairy free! We decorated this one with orange segments, but any left over blueberries or cashews would look great too!

Ingredients

- 1½ cups mixed raw nuts (almonds, brazil nuts and walnuts) (225g)
- ¾ cup pitted dates roughly chopped (120g)
- 2 cups cashews (soaked in water for an hour) (300g)
- Juice and zest of 1 orange
- ¼ cup agave syrup (55g)
- ¼ cup melted coconut oil (55g)
- Juice of one lemon
- 1¾ cup blueberries (190g)

Method

- Blend nuts and dates in a food processor until mixture sticks together when pressed. Evenly press into loose-bottom cake tin.
- Blend cashews, orange and lemon juice, agave syrup and coconut oil until smooth. Add orange zest in with spoon. Put ¼ cup of this mixture aside for the topping.
- Pour the rest of mixture on top of crust and spread evenly.
- Blend blueberries and reserved mixture until creamy. Spread over the "cheese" layer and chill in fridge overnight before serving.

We'd love to hear from you!

We hope you have enjoyed these Christmas recipes.

You can find more of our Clean Eating recipes on Instagram and Facebook.

@clean__eating
/startcleaneating

Alternatively get in touch via email:
hello@clean-eating.co.uk

Use the hashtag **#startcleaneating** to share pictures of your clean Christmas cooking with us!

Coming 2016!

12 weeks to a NEW you.

A step-by-step guide to a sustainable and healthy diet.

Do you want to eat healthier, but find it hard to know where to begin? Or are you just too busy to find delicious but healthy recipes to cook for your family?

We will be introducing a 12 week plan to get you eating nutritious and delicious food. It is a gentle introduction to clean eating in a way that you can stick to.

No more fad diets!

To be the first to hear more, subscribe at:
www.clean-eating.co.uk/12weekplan

13831681R00018

Printed in Great Britain
by Amazon.co.uk, Ltd.,
Marston Gate.